# ESSENTIAL TECHNIQUE
## FOR BAND

### INTERMEDIATE TO ADVANCED STUDIES

TIM LAUTZENHEISER

JOHN HIGGINS

CHARLES MENGHINI

PAUL LAVENDER

TOM C. RHODES

DON BIERSCHENK

Student Activation Code
E3TB-0291-8903-6741

ISBN 978-0-634-04419-9

HAL•LEONARD®
CORPORATION
7777 W. BLUEMOUND RD. P.O. BOX 13819 MILWAUKEE, WI 53213

## Bb MAJOR

### 1. SCALE AND ARPEGGIO

### 2. EXERCISE IN THIRDS

### 3. ARPEGGIO STUDY

### 4. TWO-PART ETUDE

### 5. CHROMATIC SCALE

### 6. BALANCE BUILDER

**THEORY**

*divisi* or *div.*    Divide the written parts among players, usually into two parts, with equal numbers playing each part.

*unison* or *a2*    All players play the same part (usually found after a divisi section).

### 7. CHORALE

Andante

*mf*

*rit.*

3

## 8. GREAT GATE OF KIEV

Modeste Mussorgsky

## 9. CHILDREN'S SHOES

Black American Spiritual

## 10. SOUND AN ALARM

George Frideric Handel

## 11. HALLELUJAH CHORUS

George Frideric Handel

**12. RHYTHM RAP** *Clap the rhythm while counting and tapping.*

**THEORY**

**3/8 Time Signature** = **3 beats** per measure
= **Eighth** note gets one beat

♪ = 1 beat   ♩ = 2 beats   ♩. = 3 beats

3/8 time is usually played with a slight emphasis on the 1st beat of each measure. In faster music, this primary beat will make the music feel like it's counted "in 1."

**13. RHYTHM RAP** *Compare this exercise with No. 12.*

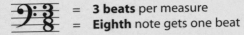

**14. WALTZ PETITE**

**15. MOLLY BANN**

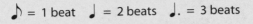
English Folksong

**THEORY**

**9/8 Time Signature** = **9 beats** per measure
= **Eighth** note gets one beat

♪ = 1 beat   ♩. = 6 beats
♩ = 3 beats
♩ = 2 beats

9/8 time is usually played with a slight emphasis on the **1st**, **4th**, and **7th** beats of each measure. This divides the measure into 3 groups of 3 beats each. In faster music, these three primary beats will make the music feel like it's counted "in 3."

**16. RHYTHM RAP** *Clap the rhythm while counting and tapping.*

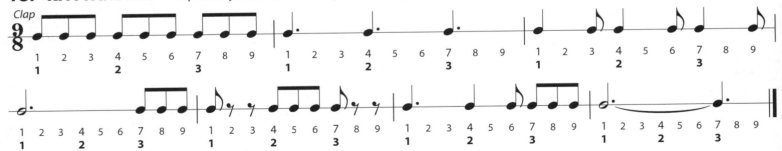

**17. SUNDAY AT NINE**

## G MINOR

## Minor Keys

Minor keys and their scales sound different from major keys because of their different pattern of whole and half steps. Each minor key is *relative* or "related" to the major key with the same key signature.

The simplest form of a minor key is called **natural minor**. Two other types are **harmonic minor** and **melodic minor**, each of which have certain altered tones.

### 18. NATURAL MINOR  *Practice both upper and lower octaves.*

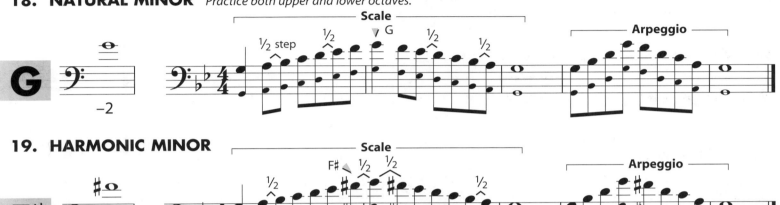

### 19. HARMONIC MINOR

### 20. PAT-A-PAN

French

### 21. THE SLEDGEHAMMER SONG

Russian

### 22. ESSENTIAL ELEMENTS QUIZ – AUSTRALIAN FOLK SONG

Australian

## E♭ MAJOR

**23. SCALE AND ARPEGGIO**

**24. EXERCISE IN THIRDS**

**25. ARPEGGIO STUDY**

**26. TWO-PART ETUDE**

**27. CHROMATIC SCALE**

**28. BALANCE BUILDER**

**29. CHORALE**

Austrian composer **Johann Strauss Jr.** (1825–1899) is also known as "The Waltz King." He wrote some of the world's most famous waltzes (dances in 3/4 meter). This waltz is from *Die Fledermaus* ("The Bat"), Strauss' most famous **operetta**. Operettas were the forerunners of today's musicals, such as *Oklahoma*, *The Sound Of Music*, and *The Phantom Of The Opera*.

## 30. ADELE'S SONG
Johann Strauss Jr.

## 31. MARINE'S HYMN

## 32. RHYTHM RAP

## 33. KEEPIN' SECRETS
Appalachian Folk Song

## 34. THE KEEL ROW
Sea Song

8

## 35. JACK'S THE MAN

**Moderately**

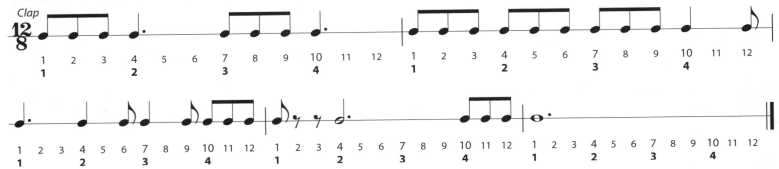

**THEORY**

**12/8 Time Signature** 𝄢 **12/8** = **12 beats** per measure / = **Eighth** note gets one beat

♪ = 1 beat    ♩. = 3 beats    ♩.♩. = 9 beats
♩ = 2 beats    ♩. = 6 beats    𝅝. = 12 beats

12/8 time is usually played with a slight emphasis on the **1st**, **4th**, **7th** and **10th** beats of each measure. This divides the measure into 4 groups of 3 beats each. These four primary beats will make the music feel like it's counted "in 4."

## 36. RHYTHM RAP    *Clap the rhythm while counting and tapping.*

## 37. SERENADE

## 38. WITH THINE EYES

**Lento** ◁ *Slowly*

*molto rit.*

△ *molto = "much"*

## C MINOR

### 39. NATURAL MINOR

### 40. HARMONIC MINOR

Even today, **Native American Indian music** continues to be an important part of tribal dancing ceremonies, using Apache fiddles, rattles, flutes, and log drums to accompany simple songs. American composer **Charles Wakefield Cadman** (1881–1946) wrote this song in 1914 based on Indian melodies he researched throughout his lifetime.

**HISTORY**

### 41. SONG OF THE WEEPING SPIRIT

Native American Indian Melody
Adapt. Charles Wakefield Cadman

### 42. SCOTTISH LEGEND

Amy Marcy Beach

### 43. ESSENTIAL ELEMENTS QUIZ  *Which measures sound major and which ones minor?*

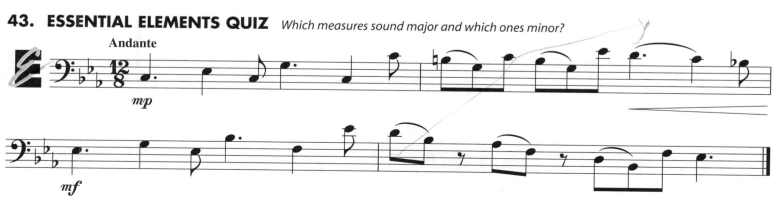

**F MAJOR**

### 44. SCALE AND ARPEGGIO   *Practice both upper and lower octaves.*

### 45. EXERCISE IN THIRDS

### 46. ARPEGGIO STUDY

### 47. TWO-PART ETUDE

### 48. CHROMATIC SCALE

D# (E♭ enharmonic)

△ G# (A♭ enharmonic)

### 49. BALANCE BUILDER

### 50. CHORALE

Andante

*mf*

*rit.*

## 51. REST ALERT

## 52. RHYTHM RAP

## 53. ISLAND SONG

## 54. THE LITTLE CHILD

Claude Debussy

**Triplets with Rests**  Triplets that start or end with a rest are usually marked with a bracket ⌐—3—⌐

**THEORY**

## 55. TRIPLET AND REST VARIATIONS

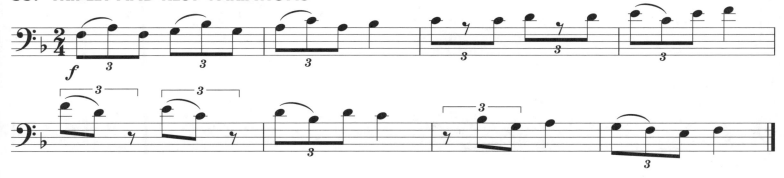

## 56. TURKEY IN THE STRAW

American Folk Song

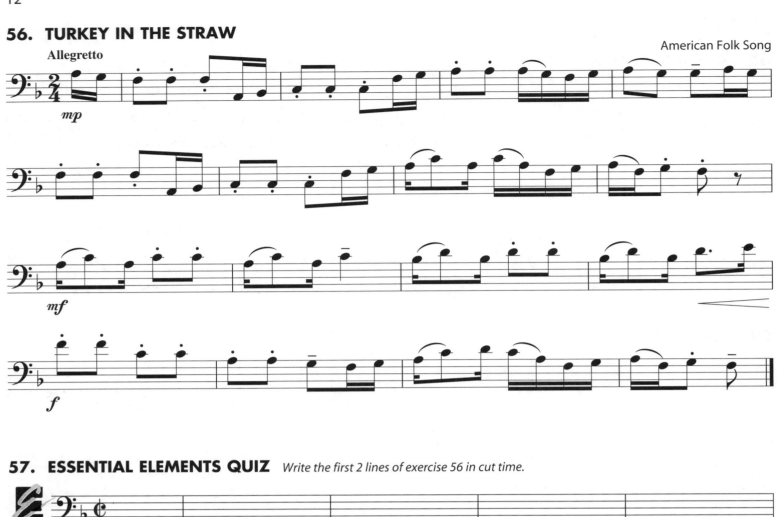

## 57. ESSENTIAL ELEMENTS QUIZ   *Write the first 2 lines of exercise 56 in cut time.*

**Sixteenth Notes and Rests** in $\frac{6}{8}, \frac{3}{8}, \frac{9}{8}, \frac{12}{8}$

| | |
|---|---|
| ♪ = ½ beat  𝄾 = ½ beat | ♩ = 2 beats  𝄾 = 2 beats |
| ♩ = 1 beat  𝄾 = 1 beat | ♩. = 3 beats  𝄾. = 3 beats |

## 58. RHYTHM RAP

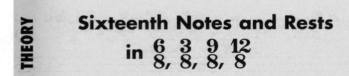

## 59. SONATINA

## D MINOR

### 60. NATURAL MINOR

### 61. HARMONIC MINOR

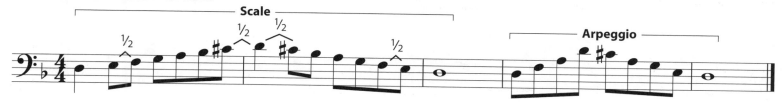

### 62. COSSACK MARCH

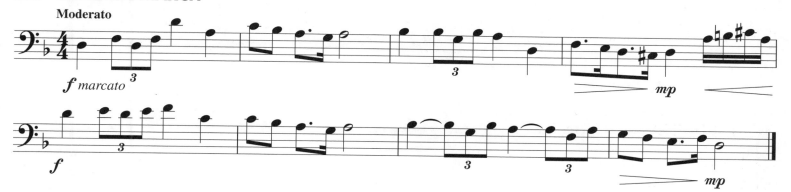

### 63. SLAVONIC DANCE NO. 2

Antonin Dvorák

### 64. ESSENTIAL ELEMENTS QUIZ – THE PRETTY GIRL

Irish

## A♭ MAJOR

### 65. SCALE AND ARPEGGIO  *Practice both upper and lower octaves.*

### 66. EXERCISE IN THIRDS

### 67. ARPEGGIO STUDY

### 68. TWO-PART ETUDE

### 69. CHROMATIC SCALE

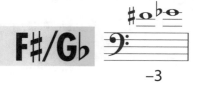

### 70. BALANCE BUILDER

### 71. CHORALE

**The Star Spangled Banner** is the national anthem of the United States of America. Francis Scott Key wrote the words during the 1814 battle at Fort McHenry. He listened to the sounds of the fighting throughout the night while being detained on a ship. At dawn, he saw the American flag still flying over the fort. He was inspired to write these words, which were later set to the melody of a popular English song.

## 72. THE STAR SPANGLED BANNER

Words by Francis Scott Key
Music by John Stafford Smith

Allegro maestoso

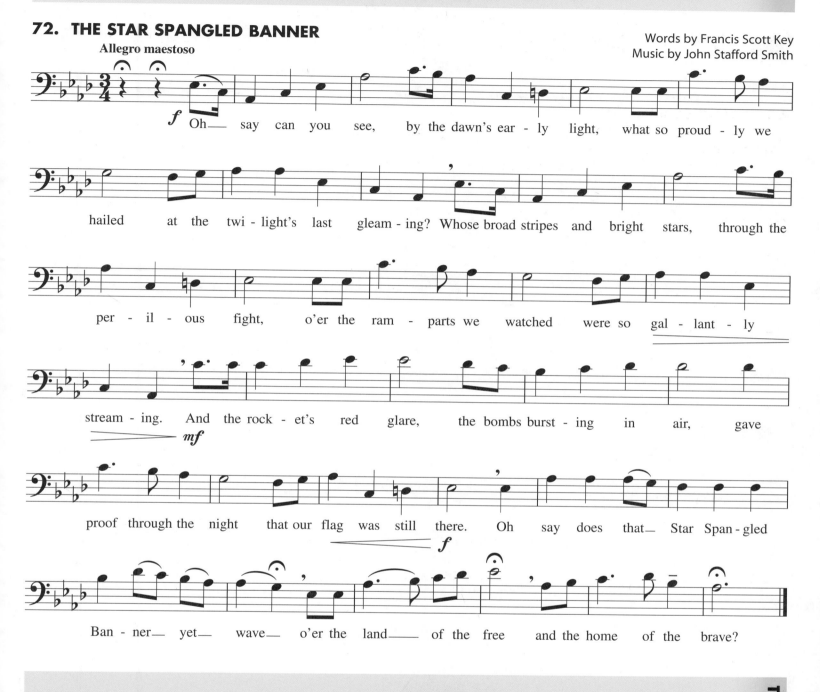

*f* Oh— say can you see, by the dawn's ear - ly light, what so proud - ly we

hailed at the twi - light's last gleam - ing? Whose broad stripes and bright stars, through the

per - il - ous fight, o'er the ram - parts we watched were so gal - lant - ly

stream - ing. And the rock - et's red glare, the bombs burst - ing in air, gave *mf*

proof through the night that our flag was still there. Oh say does that— Star Span - gled *f*

Ban - ner— yet— wave— o'er the land— of the free and the home of the brave?

## Dynamics

*pp* – *pianissimo* (play very softly)    *ff* – *fortissimo* (play very loudly)
Remember to use full breath support to produce the best possible tone and intonation.

THEORY

## 73. INTERMEZZO

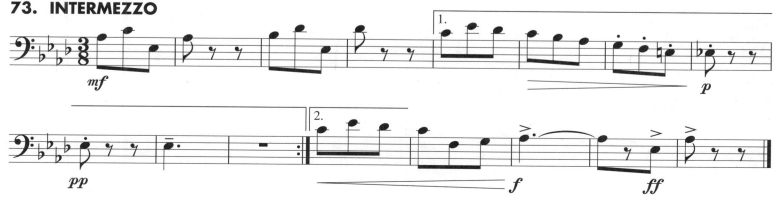

*mf*    1.    *p*

*pp*    2.    *f*    *ff*

## 74. RHYTHM RAP

## 75. MORNING STAR

## 76. SONATA

Wolfgang Amadeus Mozart

## 77. RONDEAU

Jean-Joseph Mouret

**THEORY**

**Grace Note** ♪ A small note (or notes) which is played on, or slightly before the beat.

## 78. JULIET'S WALTZ

Charles Gounod

# F MINOR

### 79. NATURAL MINOR  *Practice both upper and lower octaves.*

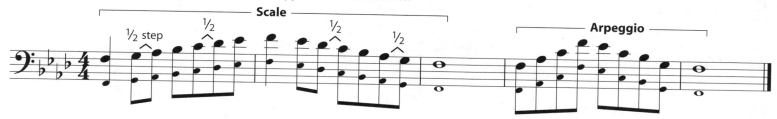

### 80. HARMONIC MINOR

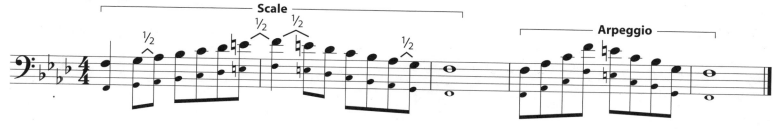

### 81. SORCERER'S APPRENTICE

Paul Dukas

### 82. I WALK THE ROAD AGAIN

American

### 83. ESSENTIAL ELEMENTS QUIZ – GREENSLEEVES

English Folk Song

18

**C MAJOR**

**Black American spirituals** originated in the 1700's. As one of the largest categories of true American folk music, these melodies were sung and passed on for generations without being written down. Black and white people worked together to publish the first spiritual collection in 1867, four years after *The Emancipation Proclamation* was signed into law.

## 91. SIT DOWN, SISTER

Black American Spiritual

## 92. SPINNING SONG – Duet

Johann Ellmenreich

## Quarter Note Triplets

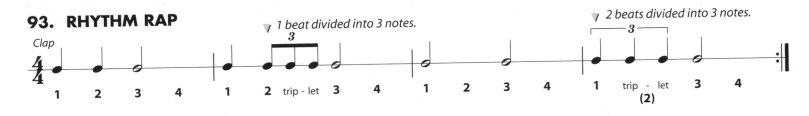

Similar to eighth note triplets where 1 beat is divided into 3 equal notes,  quarter note triplets divide 2 beats into 3 equal notes.

---

### 93. RHYTHM RAP

---

### 94. THREE FOR TWO

---

### 95. SURIRAM'S SONG

Malaysian Folk Song

---

**HISTORY**

Africa is a large continent that is made up of many nations, and **African folk music** is as diverse as its many cultures. Folk songs from any country are expressions of work, love, war, sadness and joy. This song is from Tanzania. The words describe a rabbit hopping and running through a field. Listen to the percussion section play African-sounding drums and rhythms.

---

### 96. JIBULI (The Rabbit's Song)

Adapted Tanzanian Folk Song

**A MINOR**

### 97. NATURAL MINOR

### 98. HARMONIC MINOR

## Meter Changes

Meter changes, or changing time signatures within a section of music, are commonly found in contemporary music. Composers use this technique to create a unique rhythm, pulse, or musical style.

**THEORY**

### 99. TIME ZONES

Important French composers of the late 19th century include **Claude Debussy** (1862–1918), **Gabriel Fauré** (1845–1924), **Erik Satie** (1866–1925), **César Franck** (1822–1890), **Camille Saint-Saëns** (1835–1921), and **Paul Dukas** (1865–1935). Their works continue to have influence on the music of modern day composers. Gabriel Fauré wrote *Pavanne* (originally for orchestra) in 1887, two years before the Eiffel Tower was completed in Paris.

**HISTORY**

### 100. PAVANNE

Gabriel Fauré

## D♭ MAJOR

### 101. SCALE AND ARPEGGIO

### 102. EXERCISE IN THIRDS

### 103. ARPEGGIO STUDY

### 104. TWO-PART ETUDE

### 105. CHROMATIC SCALE

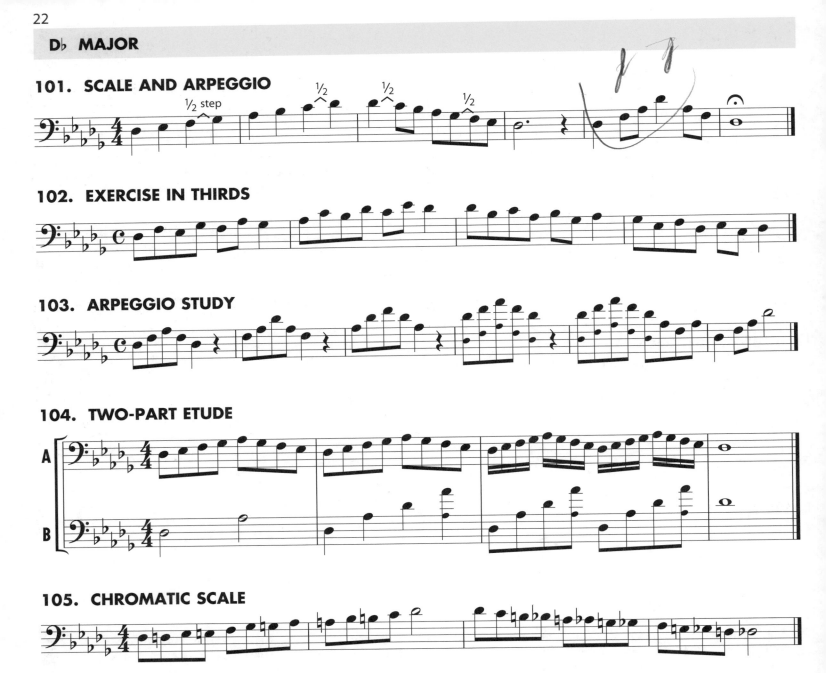

### 106. BALANCE BUILDER

### 107. CHORALE

23

## 108. GERMAN NATIONAL ANTHEM

Maestoso

Franz Josef Haydn

*mf*

*f*

## 109. JOY

Andante espressivo ◁ Expressively

Johann Sebastian Bach

*mp*

*rit.*

### 5/4 Time Signature

𝄢 5/4
= **5 beats** per measure
= **Quarter** note gets one beat

### Conducting

Practice conducting these five-beat patterns.

or

**THEORY**

## 110. RHYTHM RAP

Clap

5/4

1   2   &   3   4   5   1   2   3   4   5

## 111. LET'S COUNT FIVE

Moderato

5/4

*mf*

*sfz*

## 112. SUKURU ITO

African Folk Song

Moderato

## 113. WATER MUSIC

George Frideric Handel

Allegro maestoso

## 114. ESSENTIAL TECHNIQUE QUIZ – PICTURES AT AN EXHIBITION

Modeste Mussorgsky

Maestoso

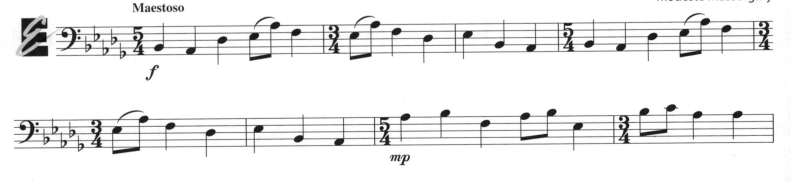

# B♭ MINOR

## 115. NATURAL MINOR

## 116. HARMONIC MINOR

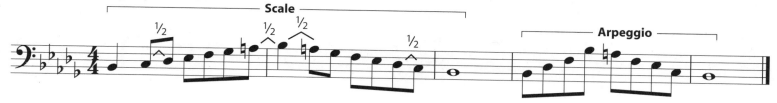

## Ostinato

THEORY

A clear and distinct musical phrase that is repeated persistently.

HISTORY

British composer **Gustav Holst** (1874–1934) is one of the most widely played composers for concert band today. Many of his compositions, including his familiar military suites, are based on tuneful English folk songs. His most famous work for orchestra, *The Planets (1916)*, has seven movements—one written for each known planet, excluding Earth. At this time, Pluto was undiscovered.

## 117. MARS – Duet/Trio

Gustav Holst

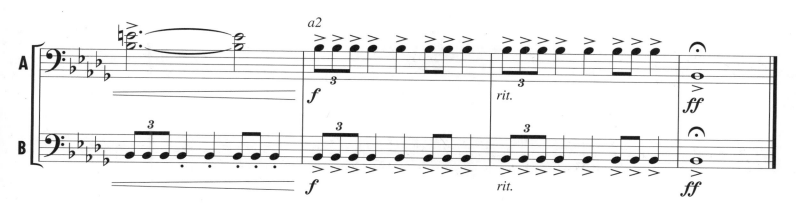

**118. SCALE AND ARPEGGIO** *Practice both upper and lower octaves.*

**119. EXERCISE IN THIRDS**

**120. ARPEGGIO STUDY**

**121. TWO-PART ETUDE**

**122. CHROMATIC SCALE**

**123. BALANCE BUILDER**

**124. CHORALE**

Norwegian composer **Edvard Grieg** (1843–1907) based much of his music on the folk songs and dances of Norway. During the late 19th century, composers often used melodies from their native land. This trend is called **nationalism**. Russian **Modeste Mussorgsky** (1839–1881), Czech **Antonin Dvořák** (1841–1904), and Englishman **Sir Edward Elgar** (1857–1934) are other famous composers whose music was influenced by nationalism.

HISTORY

## 125. NORWEGIAN DANCE

Edvard Grieg

## 126. FRENCH NATIONAL ANTHEM (LA MARSEILLAISE)

Rouget De L'Isle

Music written during the **Renaissance Period (1430–1600)** was often upbeat and dance-like. *Wolsey's Wilde* was originally written for the lute, an ancestor to the guitar and the most popular instrument of the Renaissance era. Modern day concert band composer Gordon Jacob used this popular song in his *William Byrd Suite,* written as a tribute to English composer William Byrd (1543–1623).

HISTORY

## 127. WOLSEY'S WILDE

Anonymous

## E MINOR

### 128. NATURAL MINOR *Practice both upper and lower octaves.*

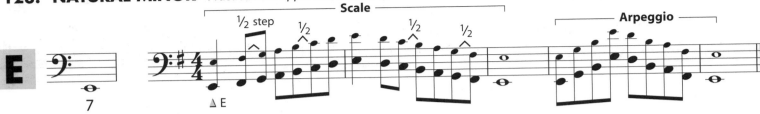

### 129. HARMONIC MINOR

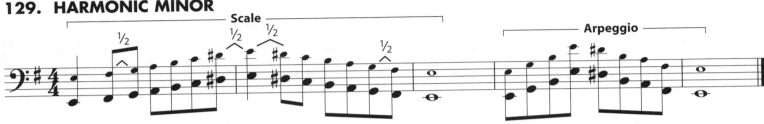

### 130. SONG OF THE SHAKUHACHI

Japanese Folk Song

**THEORY**

**D.C. al Coda**  At the **D.C. al Coda**, play again from the beginning to the indication **To Coda ⊕**, then skip to the section marked **⊕ Coda**, meaning "ending section."

**D.S. al Coda**  Similar to **D.C. al Coda**, but return to the sign 𝄋.

### 131. POLOVETZIAN DANCES

Alexander Borodin

## D MAJOR

### 132. SCALE AND ARPEGGIO

### 133. EXERCISE IN THIRDS

### 134. ARPEGGIO STUDY

### 135. TWO-PART ETUDE

### 136. CHORALE

## B MINOR

### 137. NATURAL MINOR

### 138. HARMONIC MINOR

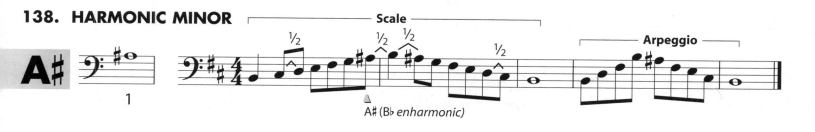

A# (Bb enharmonic)

30

**Latin American Music** combines the folk music from South and Central America, the Carribean Islands, American Indian, Spanish, and Portuguese cultures. Melodies are often accompanied by drums, maracas, and claves. Latin American music continues to influence jazz, classical, and popular styles of music. *Cielito Lindo* is a Latin American love song.

### 139. CIELITO LINDO

C. Fernandez

Tchaikovsky, along with Wagner, Brahms, Mendelssohn, and Chopin, helped define the musical era known as the **Romantic Period (1825–1900)**. The "symphonic tone poem" from this period continues to be one of the most popular musical forms performed by orchestras and bands today.

### 140. WALTZ IN FIVE (from SYMPHONY NO. 6)

Peter I. Tchaikovsky

### 141. THE YOUNG CHEVALIER

Scottish

## G♭ MAJOR

### 142. SCALE AND ARPEGGIO  *Practice both upper and lower octaves.*

△ C♭ (B♮ *enharmonic*)

### 143. EXERCISE IN THIRDS

### 144. ARPEGGIO STUDY

### 145. TWO-PART ETUDE

### 146. CHORALE

## E♭ MINOR

### 147. NATURAL MINOR

### 148. HARMONIC MINOR

# INDIVIDUAL STUDY – Trombone

**149. STRETCHING DOWN**

*CD Track 2*

**150. STUDY IN C MAJOR**

*CD Track 3*

**151. LEGATO STUDY**

*CD Track 4*

**152. STACCATO ETUDE**

*CD Track 5*

**153. ALLEGRETTO IN CUT TIME**

*CD Track 6*

# INDIVIDUAL STUDY – Trombone

### 154. 3/8 ETUDE IN G MAJOR
*CD Track 7*

### 155. STUDY IN G MINOR
*CD Track 8*

### 156. TRIPLET WORKOUT
*CD Track 9*

### 157. ETUDE IN 12/8
*CD Track 10*

# READING SKILL BUILDERS

**158. READING SKILL BUILDER NO. 1**

*CD Track 11*

**159. READING SKILL BUILDER NO. 2**

*CD Track 12*

**160. READING SKILL BUILDER NO. 3**

*CD Track 13*

**161. READING SKILL BUILDER NO. 4**

*CD Track 14*

**162. READING SKILL BUILDER NO. 5**

*CD Track 15*

# READING SKILL BUILDERS

**163. READING SKILL BUILDER NO. 6**

*CD Track 16*

**164. READING SKILL BUILDER NO. 7**

*CD Track 17*

**165. READING SKILL BUILDER NO. 8**

*CD Track 18*

**166. READING SKILL BUILDER NO. 9**

*CD Track 19*

**167. CHORALE (Prelude from Hansel and Gretel)** *CD Track 20*

Engelbert Humperdinck
Arr. by John Higgins

**168. CHORALE (Based on a Theme by Palestrina)** *CD Track 21*

Arr. by John Higgins

**169. CHORALE (Based on a Theme by J. S. Bach)** *CD Track 22*

Arr. by John Higgins

**170. CHORALE (Based on a Theme by Tchaikovsky)** *CD Track 23*

Arr. by John Higgins

**171. CHORALE (Erhalt Uns In Der Wahrheit)** *CD Track 24*

Johann Sebastian Bach
Arr. by John Higgins

**172. CHORALE (Navy Hymn)** *CD Track 25*

John Dykes
Arr. by John Higgins

**173. CHORALE (Prelude)** *CD Track 26*

Frederic Chopin
Arr. by John Higgins

# RHYTHM STUDIES

CD Tracks 27–28

# RHYTHM STUDIES

*CD Tracks 37–38*

# THE BASICS OF JAZZ STYLE
**from Essential Elements for Jazz Ensemble**

## Accenting "2 and 4"

For most traditional music the important beats in 4/4 time are 1 and 3. In jazz, however, the emphasis is usually on beats 2 and 4. Emphasizing "2 and 4" gives the music a jazz feeling.

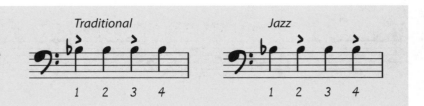

**174. ACCENTING 2 AND 4** *CD Track 47*

## Jazz Articulations

These are the four basic articulations in jazz.

 **Tenuto** (full value)

 **Staccato** (short, unaccented)

 **Long Accent** (full value, accented)

 **Roof Top Accent** (short, accented)

## Swing 8th Notes Sound Different Than They Look

In swing, the 2nd 8th note of each beat is actually played like the last third of a triplet, and slightly accented. 8th notes in swing style are usually played legato.

**175. SWING 8TH NOTES** *CD Track 48*

## Quarter Notes

Quarter notes in swing style are usually played detached (staccato) with accents on beats 2 and 4.

**176. QUARTERS AND 8THS** *CD Track 49*

**177. RUNNIN' AROUND** *CD Track 50*

## Syncopation in Jazz

When beats are played early (anticipated) or played late (delayed), the music becomes syncopated. Syncopation makes the music sound "jazzy."

### 178. WHEN THE SAINTS GO MARCHING IN – Without Syncopation *CD Track 51*

James Black and Katherine Purvis

### 179. WHEN THE SAINTS GO MARCHING IN – With Syncopation *CD Track 52*

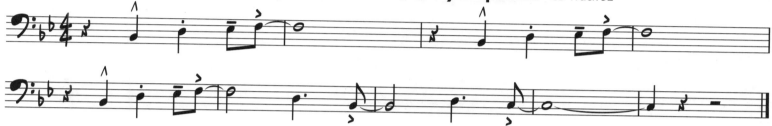

## "Jazzin' Up" the Melody by Adding Rhythms

Adding rhythms to a melody is another easy way to improvise in a jazz style. Start by filling out long notes with repeated 8th and quarter notes. Remember to swing the 8th notes (play legato and give the upbeats an accent).

### 180. "JAZZIN' UP" JINGLE BELLS *CD Track 53*

*Original Melody*

J. Pierpont

## MAKE UP YOUR OWN (IMPROVISE) *CD Track 54*

### 181. LONDON BRIDGE

Complete the melody in your own "jazzed up" way. Use only the notes shown in parentheses. Slashes on the staff indicate when to improvise.

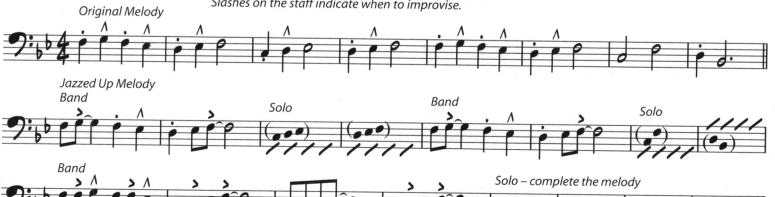

**THEORY**

## Major Scales

Play major scales as part of your daily practice routine. Play all octaves, keys, and arpeggios, at various dynamic levels and tempos. Keep a steady pulse. Try different articulation patterns, such as:

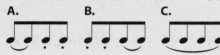

A.   B.   C.

**182. B♭ MAJOR**

*CD Track 55*

**183. E♭ MAJOR**

*CD Track 56*

**184. F MAJOR**

*CD Track 57*

**185. C MAJOR**

*CD Track 58*

**186. A♭ MAJOR**

*CD Track 59*

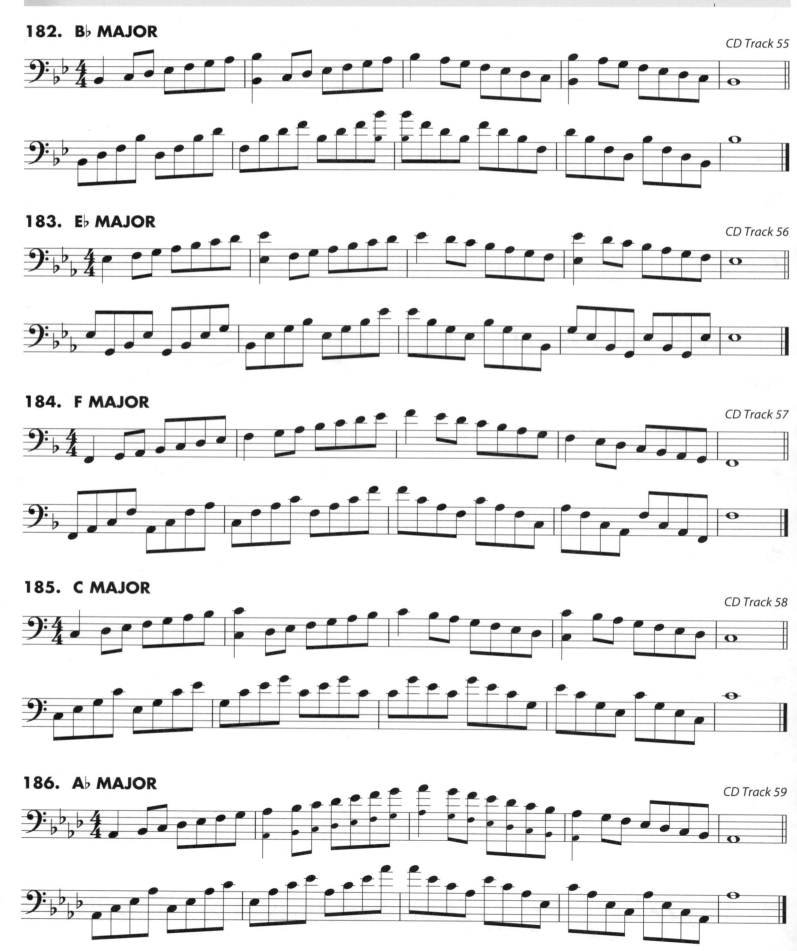

## 187. D♭ MAJOR

*CD Track 60*

## 188. G MAJOR

*CD Track 61*

## 189. D MAJOR

*CD Track 62*

## 190. A MAJOR

*CD Track 63*

## 191. G♭ MAJOR

*CD Track 64*

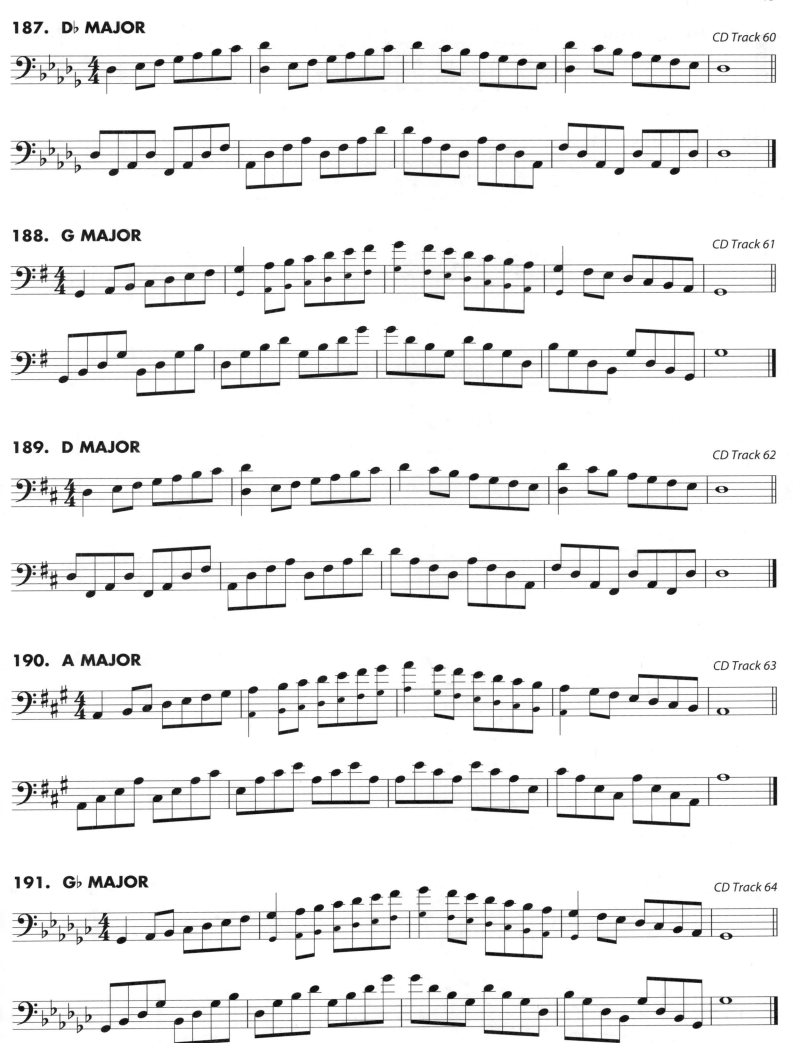

**THEORY**

## Minor Scales

Play minor scales as part of your daily practice routine. Play all octaves, all three forms and the arpeggios at various dynamic levels and tempos. Keep a steady pulse. Try different articulation patterns, such as:

### 192. D MINOR SCALE

CD Track 65

### 193. G MINOR SCALE

CD Track 66

### 194. C MINOR SCALE

CD Track 67

### 195. F MINOR SCALE

CD Track 68

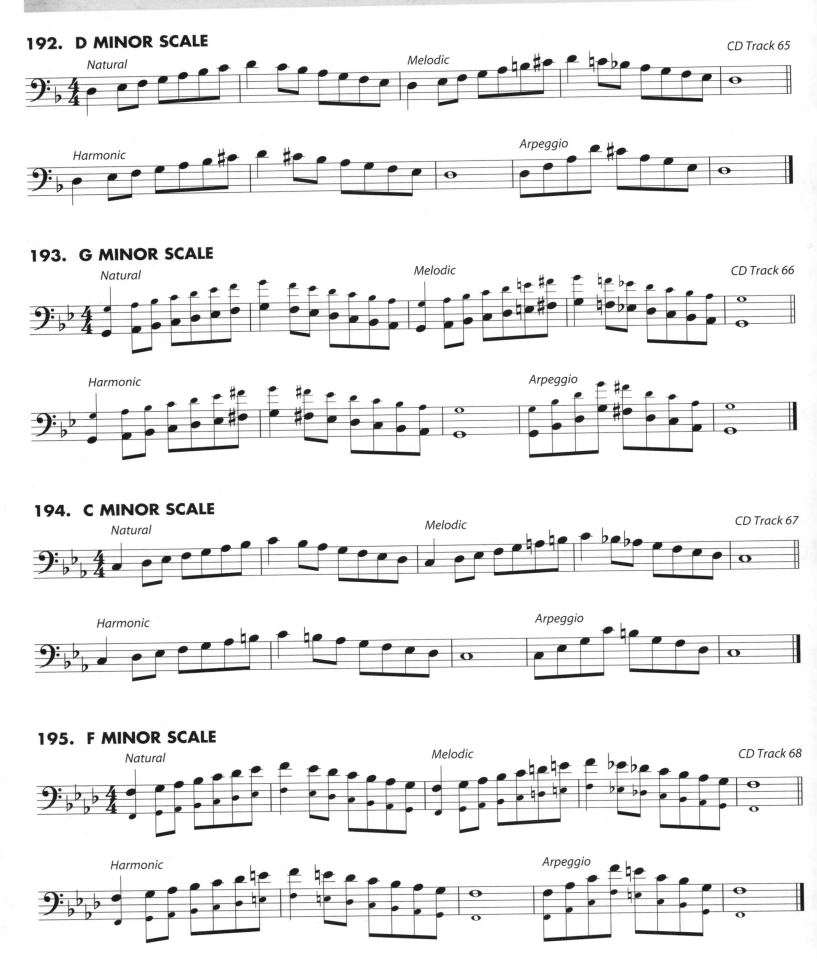

# SPECIAL EXERCISES

**LIP SLUR STUDY NO. 1**

**LIP SLUR STUDY NO. 2**

**FLEXIBILITY FUN**

# POSITION CHART

**TROMBONE**

Numbers below the notes = Slide positions

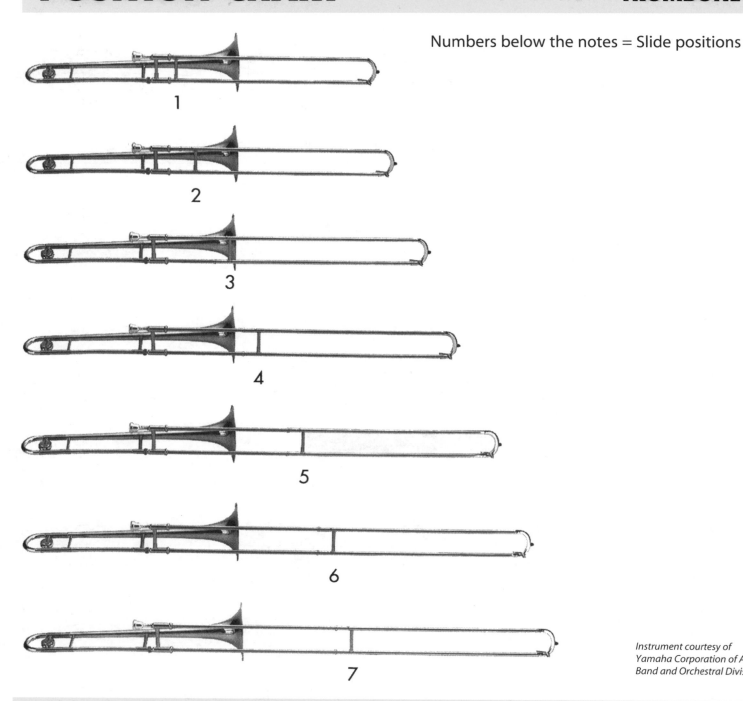

*Instrument courtesy of
Yamaha Corporation of America,
Band and Orchestral Division*

## Instrument Care Reminders

Before putting your instrument back in its case after playing, do the following:

- Use the water key to empty water from the instrument.  Blow air through it.
- Remove the mouthpiece and slide assembly.  Do not take the outer slide off the inner slide piece.  Return the instrument to its case.
- Once a week, wash the mouthpiece with warm tap water.  Dry thoroughly.

Trombone slides occasionally need oiling.  To oil your slide, simply:

- Rest the tip of the slide on the floor and unlock the slide.
- Exposing the inner slide, put a few drops of oil on the inner slide.
- Rapidly move the slide back and forth.  The oil will then lubricate the slide.
- Be sure to grease the tuning slide regularly.  Your director will recommend special slide oil and grease, and will help you apply them when necessary.

CAUTION:  If a slide or your mouthpiece becomes stuck, ask for help from your band director or music dealer.  Special tools should be used to prevent damage to your instrument.

# POSITION CHART

**TROMBONE**

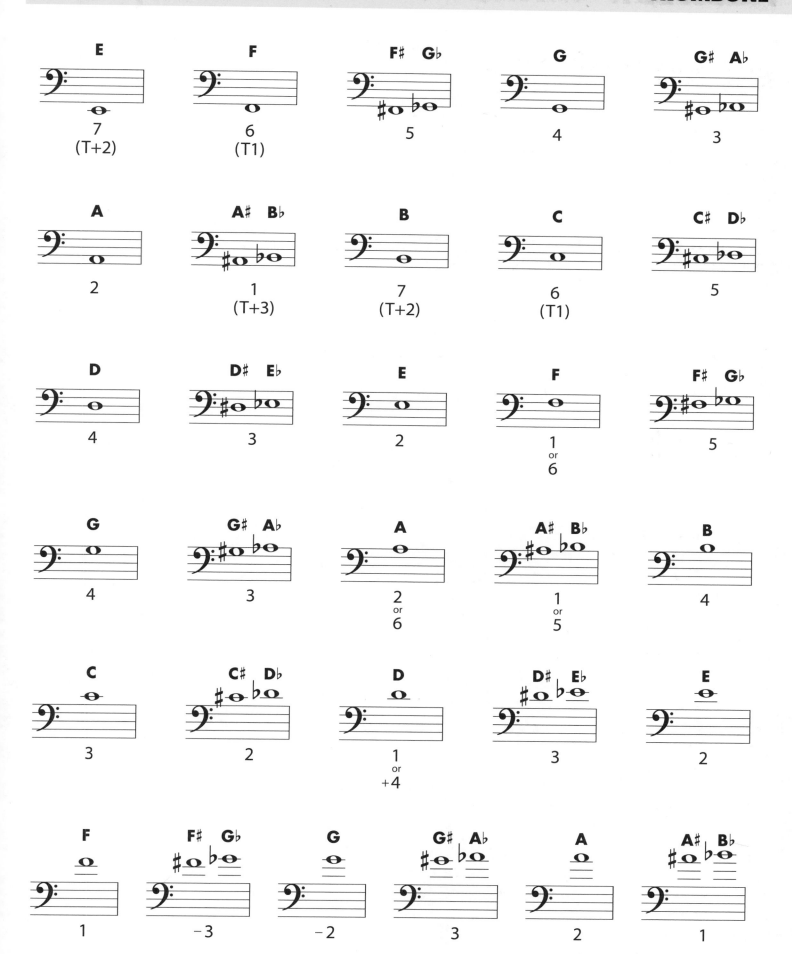

+ = Make the slide a little longer.
− = Make the slide a little shorter.
T = F Attachment "trigger."

# ◢ REFERENCE INDEX